CHAIN REACTI●NS

From
Microscopes
to Stem Cell Research

Discovering Regenerative Medicine

Sally Morgan

Heinemann
LIBRARY

www.heinemann.co.uk/library

Visit our website to find out more information about Heinemann Library books.

To order:

Phone 44 (0) 1865 888066
Send a fax to 44 (0) 1865 314091
Visit the Heinemann Bookshop at www.heinemann.co.uk/library to browse our catalogue and order online.

Produced for Heinemann Library by
White-Thomson Publishing Ltd,
Bridgewater Business Centre,
210 High Street,
Lewes, East Sussex BN7 2NH

First published in Great Britain by Heinemann Library,
Jordan Hill, Oxford OX2 8EJ, part of Harcourt Education.
Heinemann Library is a registered trademark of Harcourt
Education Ltd.

© Harcourt Education Ltd 2006
The moral right of the proprietor has been asserted.

Consultant: Professor Michael Reiss
Commissioning editor: Andrew Farrow
Editor: Kelly Davis
Design: Tim Mayer
Picture Research: Amy Sparks

Originated by RMW
Printed and bound in China by South China
Printing Company

10-digit ISBN 0 431 18593 X
13-digit ISBN 978-0-431-18593-4
10 09 08 07 06
10 9 8 7 6 5 4 3 2 1

British Library Cataloguing in Publication Data
Morgan, Sally
From microscopes to stem cell research: discovering
regenerative medicine. - (Chain reactions)
610.2'8
A full catalogue record for this book is available from the
British Library.

Acknowledgements.
The author and publisher would like to thank the
following for allowing their pictures to be reproduced in
this publication:
Corbis pp. 22 (Philippe Caron/Sygma), 28–29 (Cheque), 39
(Reuters), 46 (Ron Sachs/CNP), 51 (Ariel Skelley); NASA
p. 52; Science Photo Library pp. 1, 13 (Jim Dowdalls), 4–5
(Andrew Leonard), 6 (Dr. Jeremy Burgess), 7 (Volker
Steger), 8 (Michael Abbey), 9 (Dr. Gopal Murti), 10, 14, 27
(Eye of Science), 11 (Sinclair Stammers), 16 (Dr. P.
Marazzi), 18–19 (Klaus Guldbrandsen), 20 (Dr. Paul
Andrews), 23 (BSIP/Sercomi), 25 (Dr. Rob Stepney), 29
(Hybrid Medical Animation), 30 (Mauro Fermariello),
(BSIP/Astier), 33 (Pasquale Sorrentino), 34 (University of
Wisconsin-Madison), 35 (James King-Holmes), 36–37
(Hank Morgan), 40 (Alexis Rosenfeld), 41 (Cristina
Pedrazzini), 42 (Zephyr), 44 (John Bavosi), 45 (SPL), 47 (C.
Pouedras/Eurelios), 48 (Will and Deni McIntyre), 49
(Steve Gschmeissner), 53 (Tony Craddock), 54 (Penny
Tweedie), cover (Professor Miodrag Stojkovic).

Artwork: William Donohoe pp. 15, 21, 26; Wooden Ark
p. 12.

Cover design by Tim Mayer.

Contents

Any words appearing in the text in bold, **like this**, are explained in the Glossary.

The wonder cells

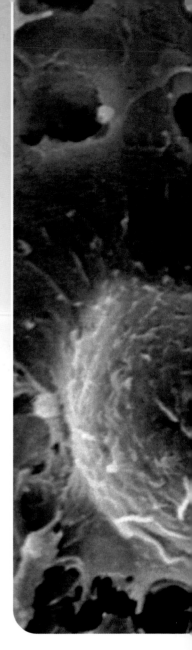

Imagine your blood **cells** being turned into muscles, or your skin cells into brain cells. Or perhaps a new liver could be made from your bone marrow? Even better, imagine your fat changing into muscle. This may all sound a bit far-fetched now. But in the future it may all be possible, thanks to the amazing discoveries in **regenerative medicine**.

Stem cells

Regenerative medicine is quite a new field of medicine. It involves replacing damaged body parts by transplanting cells into the body. At the centre of this new field of medicine is a special type of rounded cell called a **stem cell**. Stem cells have been described as "shape shifters" because they have the ability to change into other types of cell. Stem cells are found in both **embryos** and adults. In an embryo, a stem cell can turn into any type of cell – for example, a heart cell, skin cell, or brain cell. In an adult, the role of the stem cell is to repair and replace damaged cells.

Treating disease

Because stem cells can change into other types of cell they have the potential to treat many diseases, including Parkinson's disease, **Alzheimer's**, diabetes, and cancer. Stem cells could be changed into the cell type that is damaged in a particular disease. Then they could be transplanted into the affected area. Eventually they may also be used to regenerate organs, reducing the need for organ **transplants**. This is why they play such an important role in regenerative medicine.

In this book you will learn about the remarkable chain of events that began with the first observation of cells back in the 1660s. Now scientists can grow and use stem cells in the laboratory. They are also discovering many ways in which stem cells may be used in the future.

This is a stem cell in the **bone marrow**, seen using an **electron microscope**. Stem cells are small, rounded cells, with none of the special features often seen in other cells. This stem cell will divide to form new blood cells.

TALKING SCIENCE

"Stem cells are like little kids who, when they grow up, can enter a variety of professions. A child might become a fireman, a doctor or a plumber, depending on the influences in their life or environment. In the same way, these stem cells can become many tissues by making certain changes in their environment."
Dr Marc Hedrick, University of California, Los Angeles, USA

The coming of the microscope

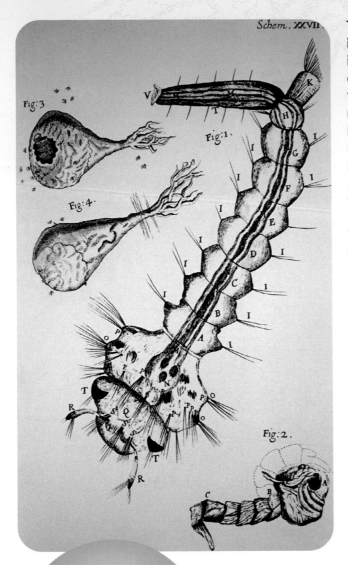

Schem. XXVII.

Fig:3

V

K

Fig:1.

H

L

I

G

I

F

I

Fig:4.

I

E

I

I

D

I

I

C

I

B

I

P

O

A

I

N

T

P

O

R

S

P

O

T

R

Fig:2.

A

B

C

This drawing of the larva of a gnat (a small biting insect) is one of many in Robert Hooke's book, *Micrographia*, published in 1665.

The first and most important step in the chain of discoveries leading to **regenerative medicine** was the invention of the microscope. Without microscopes, it would not have been possible to look at **cells**.

The first microscope was probably built by the Dutchman, Zacharias Janssen, in about 1595. It was simply a tube with a glass **lens** at each end. Early microscopes only made objects look between three times and nine times larger.

Seeing cells for the first time

Using a simple microscope, the Englishman Robert Hooke was the first person to see a cell. Hooke improved the microscope so that it was more powerful and he could see greater detail. During the early 1660s, he looked at tiny slivers of cork taken from the bark of an oak tree. He could see lots of tiny rectangular blocks which he called cells. In 1665, he published his famous book, *Micrographia*, in which he used the term "cell" for the first time.

This is one of Anton van Leeuwenhoek's first microscopes and it looks nothing like a modern **light microscope**. There is a single lens fixed between a pair of metal plates. The specimen is placed under the lens and there is a device for adjusting its height. The whole microscope is only around 100 mm (40 inches) long.

height-adjusting mechanism

lens

plates

Discovering "animalcules"

Inspired by Hooke's book, the Dutch scientist Anton van Leeuwenhoek started to build his own microscopes, trying out different types of lenses to see which was best. Many of his microscopes could magnify an object up to 270 times. It is possible that a few could magnify objects up to 500 times.

One summer, he collected water from a local lake that had turned a cloudy green. Looking at a water sample through his microscope, he discovered that it was full of tiny, single-celled animals, which he called "animalcules". He examined many other things with his microscopes, including red blood cells and **sperm cells**. In 1683, he also became the first person to look at **bacteria**, which he obtained from scraping his own and other people's teeth. These discoveries led to him being called "the father of microbiology". After his death, little progress was made on studying cell structure for another 180 years, until more powerful light microscopes enabled scientists to see greater detail inside the cell.

TALKING SCIENCE

Anton van Leeuwenhoek took scrapings from the mouths of old men who had never brushed their teeth. He found "*an unbelievably great company of living animalcules, swimming more nimbly than any I had ever seen up to this time. The biggest sort bent their body into curves in going forwards. Moreover, the other animalcules were in such enormous numbers, that all the water seemed to be alive.*"

Learning about cells

The light microscope opened up a new world for scientists. For the first time, they could observe some of the smallest living **organisms** and see some of the structures inside a cell. Scientists working on regenerative medicine have to understand how a cell functions before they can make one cell change into another type of cell.

One or many cells

The tiny organisms that Anton van Leeuwenhoek observed were mostly single-celled, such as **protozoa** and bacteria. In such organisms, the single cell carries out many different jobs to keep the organism alive. For example, it will take in and digest food, take in oxygen, and produce waste materials.

However, most organisms are multicellular. This means that they are made up of many different types of cell. Each type of cell is specialized. A specialized cell is suited to carrying out its particular job. For example, cells that take in food or oxygen have a large surface area. This helps them to absorb the food or oxygen more easily.

HOW CAN YOU MEASURE CELLS?

When you measure something, you probably use millimetres, centimetres, and metres. However, these lengths are far too large to deal with cells, so scientists use even smaller units. They are called microns and nanometres.

1 millimetre = 0.001 metre
1 micron = 0.000001 metre
1 nanometre = 0.000000001 metre

This single-celled organism is called an amoeba and it is less than 1 millimetre long.

The process by which a cell becomes specialized is very important in regenerative medicine. However, scientists could not understand how cell specialization worked until they had unravelled the secrets of the **nucleus** (see page 13).

Inside a cell

Anton van Leeuwenhoek could see the cell, the **membrane** that surrounds it, and its large nucleus. The cell is filled with **cytoplasm**. This is a gel-like substance, which contains very small structures. These structures are too small to be seen with a typical light microscope.

cell membrane

nucleus

These are simple cells that line the mouth, magnified about 1,000 times. They are flat cells with a rounded shape. The purple stained structure in each cell is the nucleus.

cytoplasm

Developing the electron microscope

During the 1930s and 1940s, scientists developed the electron microscope. This made it much easier to see inside cells.

Before the 1930s, scientists used light microscopes. These had glass lenses to focus a beam of light on to an object. The very best light microscope magnified an object about 2,000 times. This is not enough to see the structure of a cell in detail. To do this, scientists have to magnify a cell at least 10,000 times. Today, some electron microscopes can magnify an object by more than a million times.

THAT'S AMAZING!

Scientists can use an electron beam to write minute letters. The letters are so small that the 20 volumes of the *Oxford English Dictionary* would cover an area the size of a capital letter on this page. They would still be readable with an electron microscope.

How do electron microscopes work?

An electron microscope uses electrons, rather than light, to "see" the object. At the top of the microscope there is something like a gun that fires a stream of fast-moving electrons at the object. The stream of electrons passes between magnets.

This is a dust mite, magnified about 400 times with a scanning electron microscope. Dust mites are everywhere so it is probably best that we cannot see them!

This scientist is using a scanning transmission electron microscope. This type of microscope combines the good image contrast of a scanning electron microscope (SEM) with the high resolution of a transmission electron microscope (TEM).

The magnets act like the lenses in a light microscope, focusing the electrons on the object and magnifying the image. The electrons bounce off the object and hit a detector. This detector sends out signals that are changed into an image that you can see on a computer screen.

Two important discoveries led to the building of the first electron microscope. During the 1920s, a French scientist called Louis de Broglie learned more about the way electrons moved. Meanwhile, another scientist called Hans Busch discovered that magnets could focus an electron beam on to an object. Using this knowledge, Max Knoll and Ernst Ruska in Germany built the first **transmission electron microscope** in 1932. The first **scanning electron microscope** was built by the Englishman Sir Charles Oatley and one of his research students in 1951.

WHAT ARE ELECTRONS?

Everything, including living things like you, is made up of millions of **atoms**. An atom contains three types of particles: electrons, protons, and neutrons. The protons and neutrons are found in the nucleus (centre) of the atom. Electrons are tiny particles that move around the nucleus.

Types of electron microscope

A transmission electron microscope passes a beam of electrons through a thin slice of the object to produce an image. This type of electron microscope is useful for studying the inside of cells. A scanning electron microscope has an electron beam that scans the surface of the object to produce a three-dimensional image. This type of microscope can be used to look at the surface of cells and to work out the structure of the cell membrane.

Parts of cells?

At first it was not easy to work out what was going on inside a cell, even with the help of a powerful electron microscope. Electron microscopes were far more difficult to use than light microscopes. For this reason, the specimens had to go through a lengthy preparation process. Often this process damaged the cells and left bits on the specimens. Sometimes scientists confused the bits (known as artefacts) with structures in the cell.

Far more detail is visible using an electron microscope compared with using a light microscope. This illustration shows a cell magnified so many times that the organelles in the cytoplasm can be seen.

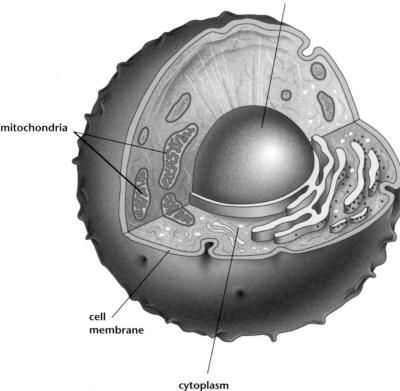

nucleus

mitochondria

cell membrane

cytoplasm

Organelles

The electron microscope showed that the cytoplasm was filled with lots of small structures. These are called **organelles**. There are several different types of organelle. Each one has a characteristic appearance and function. For example:

● the nucleus, the largest structure inside a cell, is also the cell's control centre. It is surrounded by two membranes, which have tiny holes so that **molecules** can pass into and out of the nucleus.

● the **mitochondria**, oval-shaped structures, are often referred to as the cell's power stations. They release energy that the rest of the cell can use.

WHAT ARE GENES AND CHROMOSOMES?

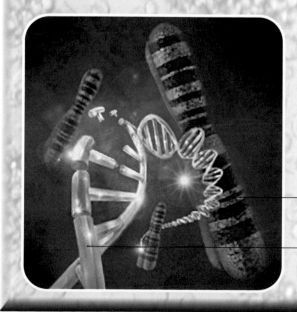

The nucleus contains genetic material in the form of **chromosomes**. There are 46 chromosomes in a typical human cell. Each chromosome is a long thread made of **DNA** (deoxyribonucleic acid), surrounded by lumps of **protein**. A **gene** is a specific length of DNA. The DNA is so long that thousands of genes are found on a single chromosome. The genes control the cell by giving instructions to the organelles. When a cell is first formed it has a complete set of genes. As it becomes specialized and its appearance changes, some of the genes are switched off because they are no longer required.

chromosome

DNA

Types of cell

There are billions of cells in the human body but they are not all the same. Each type of cell is designed to carry out a particular job. Three important types of cell in regenerative medicine are liver cells, red blood cells, and nerve cells.

Liver cells

The liver is an important organ, which has many jobs to do. For instance, it controls the amount of glucose in the blood. It also processes toxic substances, such as drugs and alcohol. The cell membrane of a liver cell has many tiny folds and this increases the surface area of the cell. This allows more materials to pass into and out of the cell.

Red blood cells

Blood is made up of cells and a liquid called **plasma**. There are three main types of blood cells floating in the plasma: red, white, and **platelets**. Most of these cells are made in the bone marrow, the spongy filling found in the centre of the body's large bones (see illustration, page 26).

The most numerous type of cell is the red blood cell, first observed by Anton van Leeuwenhoek (see page 7). The red colour comes from a substance called **haemoglobin**. As blood flows through the lungs, the haemoglobin inside the red blood cells picks up oxygen and carries it to the cells.

Red blood cells have a short life of about 120 days, so they do not need a nucleus, Instead, the middle is sunken and the cell looks a bit like a doughnut. This also leaves more space to fill with haemoglobin.

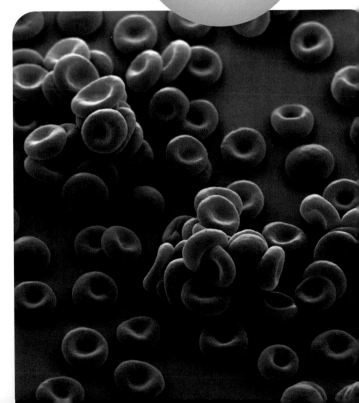

These red blood cells have no nucleus and this gives them a sunken appearance. Their red colour comes from haemoglobin.

Nerve cells

Humans have a network of nerve cells that criss-cross the body, carrying information to and from the brain. A specialized nerve cell's structure is suited to its role of carrying electrical messages. The nucleus is located in the cell body. Extending from this cell body are long thin fibres of cytoplasm. The long fibre is called an **axon**, while the shorter ones are called **dendrites**. Knowing how the different nerve cells work helps doctors understand diseases such as multiple sclerosis and Parkinson's disease.

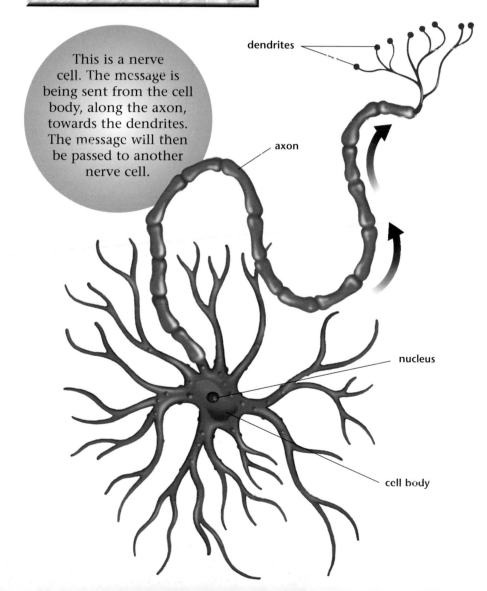

This is a nerve cell. The message is being sent from the cell body, along the axon, towards the dendrites. The message will then be passed to another nerve cell.

dendrites

axon

nucleus

cell body

Learning about stem cells

For more than 100 years, scientists had wondered how the **cells** inside an **embryo** could give rise to all the different specialized cells that make up an **organism**'s tissues and organs. The breakthrough came in 1953, when an American scientist, Roy Stevens, discovered **stem cells** in cancerous growths on mice.

Swollen monsters

Stevens was doing some research involving mice. One day he noticed that one of the male mice had an enlarged testis (the organ where sperm are made). The swelling was caused by a cancerous growth called a teratoma (the Greek word for "swollen monster"). Most cancerous growths (**tumours**) are made up of one type of cell, but teratomas are made up of many different cell types. A teratoma can contain bits of muscle, bone, skin and, in rare cases, even one or two teeth.

This X-ray of a woman's abdomen shows a dermoid cyst containing a tooth. A dermoid cyst looks similar to a teratoma but it is a fairly harmless growth.

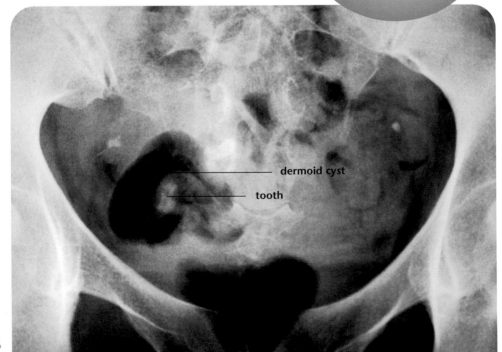

dermoid cyst

tooth

Stevens studied the teratoma under the microscope and discovered some small, round, plain cells in the middle. He called them embryonic cells but they would later become known as stem cells. In 1967, two other scientists, Barry Pierce and Lewis Kleinsmith, proved that all the different cell types in a teratoma arose from a single stem cell.

Making specialized cells

By 1970, scientists could keep these stem cells alive in a dish. If they were given the right nutrient mixture, in a special solution or **medium**, they would keep dividing. Although these stem cells had been taken from a tumour, they were very similar to embryonic cells. This research gave scientists some clues about the process going on in an embryo.

By 1973, Gail Martin and Martin Evans, working in London, could get the tumour stem cells to turn into other types of cell. By changing the medium in which the cells were growing, they could either make them divide and produce more stem cells, or they could make them change into different specialized cells, such as muscle, bone, nerve, and skin cells.

At this point, scientists realized that these cells could be very useful. They could imagine a time when doctors could repair the human body using embryonic cells. At the same time, other scientists were working in the new field of **regenerative medicine**, and human organ **transplants** were being carried out successfully.

WHAT ARE TISSUES AND ORGANS?

Tissues are made up of groups of similar cells that do the same job, such as muscle tissue or liver tissue. Tissues are grouped together to form an organ, such as a heart or a kidney. An organ has a specific role to play, and there may be several different types of tissue all working together in a single organ.

Mysterious stem cells

Scientists had thought that there were cells in the **bone marrow** that could make blood cells. But nobody had been able to identify and isolate these cells. The mystery continued until the 1960s. Then two Canadian scientists, Ernest McCulloch and James Till, made an extremely important discovery.

Mice are often used for research for several reasons. They are genetically quite similar to humans. They are small and inexpensive to keep. Also, their short lifespan and rapid breeding rate enable scientists to study disease processes in many individuals throughout their life cycle.

"For myself, there was a large element of simply chance and good luck that I got involved. In a way, for me, it's been kind of like winning a scientific lottery. I can't claim anything more than good luck, plus a prepared mind that helped us to develop research in what turned out to be such fruitful directions."
James Till, in 2005, talking about how he started investigating stem cells 40 years earlier

Bone marrow transplants

Most blood cells are made in the bone marrow, which is found in the middle of the larger bones in the body. In the early 1960s, McCulloch and Till were working on a project that they hoped would lead to new cancer treatments. From their work using mice, they knew that radiation treatment destroyed the cells in the bone marrow. However, if a mouse received a bone marrow transplant after the radiation treatment its body was able to make new blood cells. The two scientists wanted to find out why this happened.

McCulloch and Till carried out many experiments. The mice were given radiation treatment to kill the cells in their bone marrow. Then some of them were given bone marrow transplants. The breakthrough came one Sunday afternoon when McCulloch was looking for differences between the mice. The only difference he could see was that some mice had small white lumps on their **spleen**. In a mouse the spleen is found near the liver. Along with the bone marrow, it is an important site of blood cell production. Sensing that this was important, McCulloch started counting the lumps. Amazingly, the number of lumps corresponded to the amount of bone marrow they had been given. The more bone marrow they had, the greater the number of lumps. There was a lot more research to be done but this was an exciting start.

Finally, in 1963, McCulloch and Till were ready to publish their results. They revealed that bone marrow transplants worked because the bone marrow contained a special type of cell. This cell could divide to form more cells of the same type, which could then turn into all three types of blood cells. The special cells were stem cells. This discovery helped other scientists who were working on human bone marrow transplants.

Self-renewal

Unlike a red blood cell or a muscle cell, a stem cell does not have any specialized features. However, stem cells can divide and produce copies of themselves again and again. This process is called self-renewal and continues throughout the life of an organism.

In contrast, specialized cells, such as those in the blood and muscle, do not normally divide and copy themselves. If they are seriously damaged by disease or injury, they cannot make replacements. But stem cells can. Stem cells can also produce many different types of cell. As well as being able to renew themselves, stem cells can form specialized cells such as blood cells and muscle cells.

This cell, seen under a microscope, is dividing.

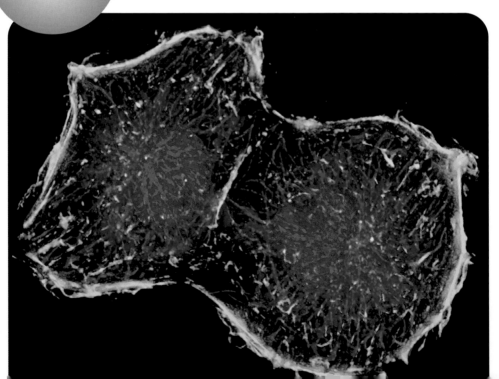

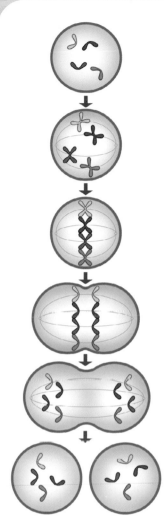

1. The nucleus contains four chromosomes.

2. Each chromosome copies itself to form two identical threads called chromatids. The nucleus disappears and a structure called the spindle appears.

These diagrams show the sequence of events that takes place in a nucleus which is dividing.

3. The chromosomes line up along the centre of the spindle.

4. The chromatids are pulled apart and move to opposite ends of the spindle.

5. The nucleus divides. Then the rest of the cell (not shown) divides.

6. The two daughter cells are identical to each other and to the parent cell. They all have the same number of chromosomes.

HOW DO STEM CELLS DIVIDE?

Like other types of cell, stem cells divide by a process called **mitosis**. In this process the parent cell splits to form two identical daughter cells. First, the nucleus starts to divide. As this happens, the chromosomes become visible as threads or chromatids. At this stage each chromosome is made up of two identical chromatids, joined together at one point. The chromosomes move to the middle of the cell, where they line up. Then they move apart, each chromatid going in the opposite direction. Finally the **cytoplasm** divides, and the two new, identical cells are formed.

Transplants and immunity

During the 1950s scientists had shown that mice with **bone marrow** diseases could be treated with bone marrow **transplants** taken from healthy mice. Scientists then tried to transplant bone marrow from one human to another but all the early attempts failed. Finding a way to transplant bone marrow successfully was a major breakthrough in medical science.

Understanding the immune system

Scientists could not transplant bone marrow and other organs successfully until they had learned about the **immune system**. The first important step forward was taken in 1958 by Frenchman Jean Dausset, who was working for the French blood **transfusion** service. He discovered that each person has specific types of **proteins** on the surface of their white blood **cells**. These proteins, called **antigens**, are unique to that person.

Jean Dausset was a transplant pioneer. His work on the immune system allowed transplant surgery to develop.

Blood contains far fewer white blood cells than red blood cells. The white blood cells swallow up any bacteria that they find in the body.

HOW DOES YOUR IMMUNE SYSTEM WORK?

Your body has amazing protection in the form of your immune system. Each day you breathe in millions of germs, such as **bacteria** and viruses, and eat many more. But you do not normally get ill because your immune system protects you. The white blood cells are the most important part of this system. They circulate around your body looking for germs. There are different types of white cells. Some swallow up germs that they find. Others produce chemicals, called antibodies, which attack the germs.

The immune system uses the antigens to identify the cells belonging to that person's body. When the immune system comes across antigens it does not recognize, it creates **antibodies** and other substances to destroy the cells that bear the foreign antigen.

Stem cells also have antigens on their surface. This means that any stem cell injected into a patient is as likely to be rejected as a transplanted organ. One way to avoid the problem of **rejection** is to use the patient's own stem cells.

First successful transplants

Dr. E. Donnall Thomas, in the United States, first started working on a cure for **leukaemia** (a type of blood cancer) in the 1950s. Many other scientists thought he would never succeed. He treated these patients by destroying their diseased bone marrow using **radiation** treatment. Then he transplanted some healthy bone marrow, taken from a twin or close relative. His research has transformed the lives of many patients. Today, 50 to 90 per cent of people diagnosed with this type of blood cancer survive.

Bone marrow transplants can be used to treat other diseases as well. In 1968, a four-month-old boy with a severe immune disorder was given a bone marrow transplant from his healthy sister. His immune system was restored and he has led a healthy life ever since. Then, in 1973, the first successful transplant took place in New York, USA, between a child and an unrelated donor. The donor, who lived in Denmark, had been found through a register of donors. The tissues of the child and those of the donor were a close match.

WHAT'S A BONE MARROW REGISTER?

There are bone marrow registers in many countries. The registers list people who are willing to donate their bone marrow. Each person on the register gives a small sample of blood. The blood is analysed, and its type is recorded on a database. When somebody needs a bone marrow transplant, doctors look on the register to find somebody whose blood type is a close match. Then that person is asked to come to a hospital where a small amount of bone marrow is removed. The world's largest registry is the National Marrow Donor Program in the United States, which was set up by the US Navy in 1986. It now has more than 5.5 million donors.

Transplanting bone marrow

The donor is given a general anaesthetic so they do not feel any pain. Then, in the operating theatre, a needle is used to remove marrow from one of the large bones. This does not leave a scar. However, the donor often feels some discomfort and will usually spend at least 24 hours in hospital.

A bone marrow transplant is very different from other types of organ transplant. The patient does not have to be operated on to receive the new marrow. It is fed into the body through a blood vessel, just like a blood transfusion. The stem cells find their way to the bone marrow in the bones. If all goes well, the stem cells will settle and start producing new blood cells within two to four weeks.

Rejection problems

When tissues or organs are transplanted into the body of another person, the immune system recognizes the antigens as being foreign. This causes the body to fight the transplant and reject it. In the early days, bone marrow transplants only took place between people who were closely related. This greatly reduced the chances of rejection. Nowadays most transplants are between people who are not related, so doctors have had to develop drugs that can stop rejection. However, the patients have to take these drugs for life. If they stop, their immune systems will start to fight the transplanted cells.

Marrow is sucked out from the donor's bone marrow, using a large needle. It is then collected and treated with a drug to stop it from clotting.

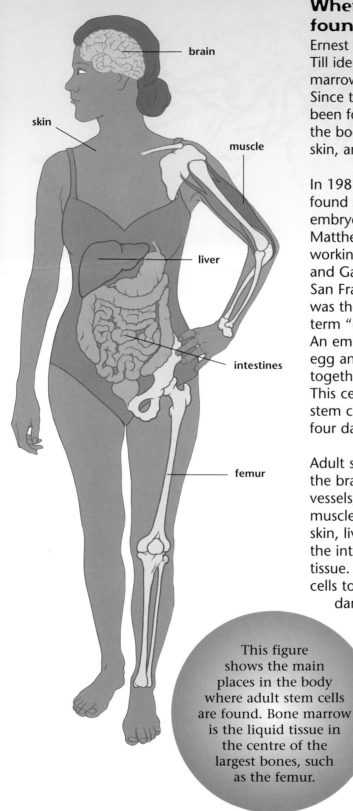

brain

skin

muscle

liver

intestines

femur

This figure shows the main places in the body where adult stem cells are found. Bone marrow is the liquid tissue in the centre of the largest bones, such as the femur.

Where are stem cells found?

Ernest McCulloch and James Till identified stem cells in bone marrow in 1963 (see page 20). Since then, stem cells have been found in other parts of the body, including the liver, skin, and intestines.

In 1981, two research teams found stem cells in mouse embryos. Martin Evans and Matthew Kaufman were working in Cambridge, UK, and Gail Martin had returned to San Francisco, USA. Gail Martin was the first person to use the term "embryonic stem cells". An embryo is formed when an egg and a **sperm cell** fuse together to form a new cell. This cell starts to divide, and stem cells form after about four days.

Adult stem cells can be found in the brain, bone marrow, blood vessels, skeletal muscle (the muscle that moves bones), skin, liver, and the lining of the intestines, as well as in fat tissue. An adult needs stem cells to replace cells that get damaged or have died. Stem cells have also been found in the **umbilical cord** that links an unborn baby with its mother's **placenta** in the **uterus** (see page 31).

This is a cross-section through human skin, magnified about 100 times. A hair (upper centre) is growing from the surface. The top layer is made up of flattened, dead skin cells. These are continuously replaced by cells from the living layer below (shown in red).

Bone marrow

Bone marrow stem cells can form several types of blood cells. These include red blood cells that carry oxygen, white cells that fight infection, and **platelets** that are involved in blood clotting. Without bone marrow, and the white blood cells that it produces, your immune system would not work.

Skin

Your skin loses cells all the time so it needs a continual supply of new cells. Your skin also needs to repair itself if it is damaged by injuries. There is a layer of stem cells just under the surface of your skin. These cells continually divide to form new cells. As this happens, the cells are pushed upwards, towards the surface of your skin. You can see this for yourself. For example, if you get a blister, new skin forms underneath the blister.

HOW DOES YOUR LIVER REPAIR ITSELF?

Your liver has an extraordinary ability to repair itself. Any damaged part of the liver can be safely removed because the stem cells in the rest of the liver will divide and replace the lost tissue. When somebody receives a liver transplant they are not given the whole liver, but just a part of a liver. The transplant normally comes from somebody who has died but it can be a living donor. This way, the liver can be used to treat several patients.

Embryonic stem cells

Embryos are an important source of stem cells. In order to carry out their experiments, scientists working on stem cell research need to understand how an embryo develops. The study of embryos, called embryology, goes back thousands of years. One of the first people to study chicken embryos was the famous philosopher Aristotle who lived in ancient Greece.

Ball of cells

An embryo is formed from a single fertilized egg cell. This cell divides into two identical cells. These cells divide again to form four cells, and again to form eight cells, and so on. The division takes place every 20 hours or so.

Identical twins are natural clones.

WHAT ARE CLONES?

Clones are cells or organisms that are identical to each other in every way. Clones form naturally – for example, identical twins. Identical twins are formed when an embryo divides into two parts, and each part grows into a new baby. Clones can also be created in the laboratory using embryos. One way to create a clone is to copy the way identical twins are formed. Scientists take an embryo that is up to four days old. They pull the ball of cells into two parts. Each part may then grow into a new individual. The individuals will be clones of each other.

This four-day-old human embryo is a hollow ball of cells. At this stage, the embryo would embed itself in the wall of the uterus (womb).

In the early stages, all the cells are identical. Any one of these cells has the potential to develop into an entire human being.

After about four days, the cells start to change and move around. The embryo is now a hollow ball of cells about the size of a pinhead.

There are two groups of cells. One group forms an outer layer. These cells go on to develop into the placenta and the umbilical cord. The other group forms a cluster of stem cells inside the hollow ball. It is this cluster that interests the scientists. They harvest the stem cells from embryos that are between five and six days old. Once this is done, the embryo dies.

If left as they are, the embryonic stem cells can divide to form more stem cells. Sometimes an embryonic stem cell divides unequally. One of the cells may develop into a specialized cell (such as a blood cell or muscle cell), while the other cells remain stem cells. The specialized cells develop into tissues.

This container holds fat and blood removed during liposuction. In liposuction operations, doctors insert a large needle into the patient's fatty tissue. They then remove the excess fat using suction. The fat contains stem cells.

Adult stem cells

Adult stem cells behave differently from embryonic stem cells. They do not divide and form lots more cells. Instead, they lie quietly in the tissues. They simply exist and do nothing until the tissue in which they are lying is damaged. For example, the tissue may be damaged by disease or injury and need to be repaired. At this point, the stem cells become active and start dividing.

As a person's body gets older, the number of stem cells decreases. Adult stem cells seem less eager than embryonic stem cells to divide and form specialized cells. This means that they are less useful to scientists than embryonic ones.

In the last few years, researchers have found adult stem cells in many more tissues. In April 2001, scientists at the University of California, Los Angeles, and the University of Pittsburgh found stem cells in fat. The fat had been sucked out of patients undergoing **liposuction** (cosmetic surgery to remove excess fat). Since millions of liposuction procedures are carried out each year, this could be a good source of adult stem cells.

Stem cells and pregnancy

In 2005, Colin McGuckin and Nico Forraz of Kingston University in Surrey, UK, found stem cells in blood within the umbilical cord. A few months later, Stephen Strom and Yoshio Miki, of the University of Pittsburgh, USA, found stem cells in the placenta. Using stem cells from these sources is less controversial than using embryonic stem cells (see page 37).

Stem cells from the placenta and umbilical cord blood could soon become readily available. The placenta and umbilical cord are saved after a woman gives birth to her baby. The blood is then extracted and stored in blood banks. The number of these blood banks is increasing all the time.

THAT'S AMAZING!

The stem cells in umbilical cord blood are very numerous. For example, as many as 10,000 stem cells can be extracted from one umbilical cord.

Collecting cord and placental blood is quite straightforward. The placenta is supported and a needle is inserted into the umbilical cord. The blood drains through the needle into a plastic collection bag. The blood is then frozen and stored for future use.

Embryonic versus adult stem cells

Scientists working on stem cell research have to choose whether to use embryonic or adult stem cells. To make this choice, they have to weigh up the advantages and disadvantages of each type of cell.

Embryonic stem cells can turn into all forms of cell. But adult stem cells can only be used to produce a few types of cell. It is also harder to take stem cells from a living adult than from an embryo. However, stem cells from fat, removed in liposuction operations, are proving easy to extract. In addition, adult stem cells do not survive as long as embryonic stem cells when grown in the laboratory.

Other possible problems

Another consideration is rejection. Scientists want to be able to inject stem cells into patients to repair damaged tissues. However, stem cells taken from another person would be attacked by the patient's immune system. This is exactly the same problem encountered by doctors when they carried out the first bone marrow transplants (see page 22). Any patient receiving stem cells from another person would have to take drugs for the rest of their life to stop this rejection. This problem can be avoided if stem cells are taken from the patient's own body. This is called a self-transplant.

? CAN STEM CELLS HAVE DEFECTS?

Another risk with using adult stem cells is that the cell may have genetic defects. During a person's life, the body's cells are exposed to sunlight and all sorts of chemicals. This damages some of the cells and alters the genetic information in their nuclei. As the person gets older, the amount of damage increases. This means that stem cells taken from the body of an adult could have genetic faults. This faulty information would then be passed on to the new cells.

One of the greatest concerns about the use of embryonic cell stems is their ability to keep on dividing. This is a very useful feature when new stem cells are needed in the laboratory. However, scientists are concerned that embryonic stem cells could keep multiplying when they are injected into a person's body.

This scientist is studying the nuclei of stem cells under a light microscope. The nuclei show up as white dots on the screen. Stem cells grown in a laboratory over many months can develop defects. These faults can be spotted when the cells are examined closely.

WHAT ELSE DO WE NEED TO KNOW ABOUT STEM CELLS?

A lot more knowledge is needed about stem cells and their behaviour before they can be used in transplant treatments. For example, scientists do not know why the number of stem cells in the body decreases with age and why some stop working entirely. They want to find out whether the decrease in number is due to stem cells dying and not being replaced. It is not yet known how transplanted stem cells will behave inside the body. Scientists also want to find out whether hormones interfere with the action of stem cells.

Growing stem cells

A major breakthrough in **stem cell** research occurred in 1998. Scientists needed to be able to grow human stem cells in the laboratory in order to avoid having to find fresh sources of stem cells from **embryos** and adult tissues. Two teams of scientists developed new ways of doing this in the United States. James Thomson led a research team at the University of Wisconsin-Madison, while John Gearhart's team was based at Johns Hopkins University in Baltimore. Although they used different sources of stem cells, both teams managed to grow stem cells in the laboratory.

HOW ARE STEM CELLS GROWN?

The best way to grow stem cells is to place the cells in a dish that is coated on the inside with a layer of skin cells taken from a mouse embryo. The skin cells create a sticky surface to which the stem cells can attach. The stem cells stop growing once they have formed a continuous layer over the surface of the culture dish. At this point, some of the cells have to be moved to a new dish.

Making millions of cells

James Thomson got his stem cells from donated human embryos. The embryos were grown in the laboratory for around five days. Then about 30 stem cells were taken from the embryo and transferred to a plastic culture dish that contained a culture **medium**.

James Thomson is shown here at the University of Wisconsin-Madison, USA. Thomson used human embryos to develop a line of stem cells. Cells from this line are still being used today.

Stem cells do not remain as stem cells for long. If the nutrients in the culture medium are not carefully monitored, the stem cells start changing into other cell types. The breakthrough came when the team discovered the right mix of nutrients to prevent the stem cells from changing into specialized cells. They allowed the cells to grow and divide until a mass of cells filled the plastic dish. Then some of the cells were moved to new dishes so they could continue to grow. This process was repeated many times. After about six months, there were millions of embryonic stem cells. During the study, the team had to keep testing the stem cells to prove that they had not changed in any way.

Laboratories grow stem cells to produce the large numbers needed for their research projects. The stem cells are placed in dishes, which have to be kept at the right temperature.

WHAT IS IVF?

Infertile couples can have fertility treatment in order to have a baby. The woman's eggs are placed in a plastic laboratory dish and fertilized with **sperm** to create embryos. The embryos are examined under a microscope to check that they are normal. Then an embryo is placed in the woman's **uterus** where it develops into a baby. Any spare embryos may be donated to stem cell research, such as that carried out by James Thomson's team.

The issues

Human **stem cell** research has led to a lot of discussion between scientists, politicians, and the public. It is a new field and there are many concerns about the rights and wrongs of this type of work. There have also been attention-grabbing headlines in the newspapers and some inaccurate reporting.

Concerns about embryos

The early research into stem cells involved using **embryos**. At first, the embryos were taken from animals such as frogs and then from mice and other laboratory animals. More recently, human embryos and **fetuses** (unborn babies) have been used. This worries many people.

This scientist is freezing spare embryos from an IVF treatment. If the woman does not get pregnant, she can try again at a later date, using some of the frozen embryos. However, after a successful pregnancy the woman may not want the spare embryos. She may then choose to donate them for stem cell research.

Some people feel that an embryo represents a new life and so should be given all the protection and rights of an individual. They do not believe that embryos should be produced or destroyed solely for the purposes of medical research.

Scientists involved with this research argue that most of the embryonic stem cells in use today have come from embryos that were created during **IVF** treatments (see page 35). In IVF, several embryos are normally produced at the same time. Only two or three are placed inside the woman's uterus in the hope that one will develop into a baby. Usually the spare embryos are frozen in case the procedure does not work and has to be repeated. However, if the mother gives permission, the spare embryos may be used in stem cell research.

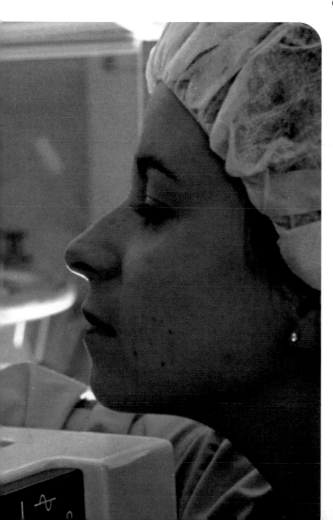

There are also concerns about the fact that the embryo dies when the stem cells are removed. However, scientists have found a way to remove the stem cells without damaging the embryo. This development may go some way towards making the research more acceptable.

Some stem cells have been taken from fetuses. These are obtained when a woman decides to end a pregnancy by having an abortion. If the woman gives permission, the stem cells are taken from fetal tissues, such as the brain and **bone marrow**.

Thanks to the pioneering work of Thomson and Gearhart (see page 34), researchers are now able to grow stem cells in the laboratory. This has reduced the need to use human embryos.

New laws

Governments have passed laws to make sure that this research is carried out properly. In the United Kingdom, researchers are allowed to work on human embryos up to 14 days in age. After this time they must be destroyed. These embryos are usually spare embryos from IVF, but the law does allow researchers to produce embryos for specific research projects. In some other European countries, researchers are permitted to use spare embryos. But embryos must never be produced simply for the purposes of research. The laws in the United States are much tougher. For example, researchers cannot get any government funding for research that involves destroying human embryos.

However, these laws and regulations do not prevent the research from being done elsewhere. Scientists can work in many other countries where there are no restrictions. Some scientists worry that the United States will fall behind in this research and there will be fewer medical advances to treat people.

Avoiding the problem

Using adult stem cells or **umbilical cord** stem cells in research avoids the restrictions that apply when using embryonic stem cells. Scientists are therefore choosing to use adult stem cells to develop new medical treatments (see page 41).

JAMES KELLY'S STORY

James Kelly had a terrible car accident in 1998. The accident left him paralysed from the waist down and unable to work. He spends 10 to 14 hours a day researching **regenerative medicine** and potential treatments for his spinal injury. He used to support embryonic stem cell research and he wrote a letter to President George W. Bush encouraging him to fund research in this field. Now he has changed his mind. As a result of his research, he is convinced that his best hope of walking again is to be found in his own adult tissues. He also believes that banning expensive research into embryonic stem cells would release more money for adult stem cell research. Then a cure for his disability might be found sooner.

The film actor Christopher Reeve, best known for playing Superman before he was paralysed in a riding accident, campaigned for stem cell research in the United States. He hoped that research into stem cells would lead to a treatment for his spinal injury. He died in 2005.

Using stem cells, especially those taken from the patient's own body, means that there is less risk of **rejection**. Most people think that research into adult cell stems is acceptable. In fact, many people are excited by the thought that their own body cells may be able to cure their diseases in the future.

TALKING SCIENCE

"*We don't have to go down long paths that will probably not lead to any cures simply for the sake of leaving no stone unturned. What we have to do is use our limited resources efficiently. Money spent on embryonic stem cell research and human cloning is money that cannot be spent on [investigating] adult stem cells. And that means that the cures that I believe are available will be slower in reaching the patients that need them.*"
James Kelly

Regenerative medicine

If a starfish loses an arm or a lizard loses its tail, it can grow a new one. In the same way, **stem cells** can replace damaged **cells** in the body. The use of stem cells to repair damaged tissues and organs is called **regenerative medicine**.

New cures

There are a number of severe diseases, such as Parkinson's disease and diabetes, for which there are no cures at present. Stem cell research could eventually lead to cures for these diseases as well as many other health problems.

This starfish is regenerating a missing leg. Regeneration enables the starfish to survive even when it is pulled into several pieces. Stem cell research could eventually lead to doctors being able to regenerate damaged parts of the human body in a similar way.

People with serious heart, lung, kidney, or liver disease may be lucky enough to be given a new organ in a **transplant** operation. However, patients often have to wait many years for an organ. Sometimes they die before one becomes available.

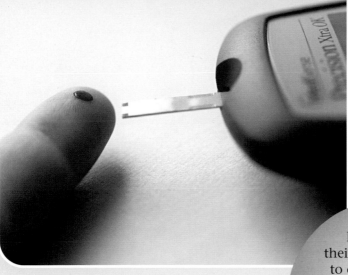

This may change in the future when doctors are able to take stem cells from a patient, grow them in the laboratory, and then inject them back into the patient. Once in the body, the stem cells would repair the damaged organ.

For example, the **pancreas** is an organ that produces insulin. Insulin is needed to control the level of glucose in the blood. If anything goes wrong with the pancreas and there is not enough insulin, the person becomes diabetic. At the moment there is no cure, so diabetics must be given insulin daily. However, stem cells could repair the pancreas and restore insulin production. Researchers have already managed to get embryonic stem cells from mice to turn into insulin-producing cells. But there is a long way to go before a treatment becomes available for people.

? WHY CAN STEM CELLS NOT BE USED TO TREAT GENETIC DISEASES?

Several diseases, such as sickle cell anaemia and cystic fibrosis, are caused by faulty **genes**. Unfortunately adult stem cells taken from the sufferers cannot be used to treat their diseases. This is because every cell in the sufferer's body has the faulty gene, including the stem cells. Stem cells taken from another person could possibly be used. But then the problem of **rejection** would have to be overcome.

narrowed arteries

This X-ray shows the narrowed arteries in a diseased heart. Blocked arteries can lead to a heart attack, which damages the heart muscle. Scientists hope to use stem cells to help repair such damage.

Stem cells and heart disease

For a long time doctors did not believe that heart cells could regenerate if they were damaged during a heart attack. Now new research suggest that stem cells may be able to repair damaged heart muscle.

HOW CAN STEM CELLS CURE BLINDNESS?

Stem cells can be used to treat patients who have damaged their **corneas** (the outer layer of the eye) and are either blind or going blind. British eye specialist Mr Sheraz Daya takes stem cells, which occur naturally in the eye, and grows them into sheets of cells in the laboratory. Then a sheet of cells is dropped on to the surface of the eye. The cells are held in place by a **membrane**. The membrane dissolves away as the cells attach themselves to the cornea. The presence of stem cells on the cornea triggers the eye to repair itself. Within a few weeks, many of the patients say that their sight has improved.

Scientists caused mice to have heart attacks. Then they injected bone marrow stem cells. Just a few weeks later, their hearts had improved and there was less damaged heart tissue. Stem cells in the heart muscle itself probably carry out repairs.

Some interesting information came from the study of a man who had received a new heart from a woman in a heart transplant operation. All the cells in a man's body contain an XY **chromosome**. Cells in a female contain XX chromosomes. Some years after the transplant, the man died and his heart was examined. Since the heart came from a woman, all the heart cells should have contained XX chromosomes.

Doctors were surprised to find that 10 per cent of the cells had XY chromosomes. How did this happen? The doctors think that stem cells had moved to the heart from other parts of the man's body.

When a patient has blocked **arteries** in their heart, the blockages prevent blood from reaching the heart muscle. This can cause a heart attack. The blocked section of artery has to be bypassed to let the blood get through. This is done by taking a length of vein from the patient's leg and using it to bypass the blocked artery.

TALKING SCIENCE

Edward Bailey lost his sight in one eye after strong acid got into his eye while he was cleaning pipes in a factory. He said that his eye operation, carried out by Mr Sheraz Daya, had transformed his life. *"It was the most emotional moment. I couldn't believe it. For ten years all I had seen was shades of black and grey. Then after I had the operation the nurse came by and I saw a flash of blue from her uniform. I went home and when I took the patch off my eye, I had my vision back. It is only when you lose something like sight that you realize how precious it is."*

Repairing the heart

American doctors are trying a new technique involving stem cells. During the operation, the doctors remove bone marrow and extract the stem cells. The stem cells are then injected into the heart. It is hoped that the stem cells will speed up the patient's recovery and help the heart to repair itself.

This illustration shows a heart that has had a triple bypass operation. The coronary arteries run over the surface of the heart. They supply oxygen to the heart muscle. There are three grafts, made from a length of vein taken from the leg. These grafts run from the aorta to the coronary arteries, bypassing the blockages.

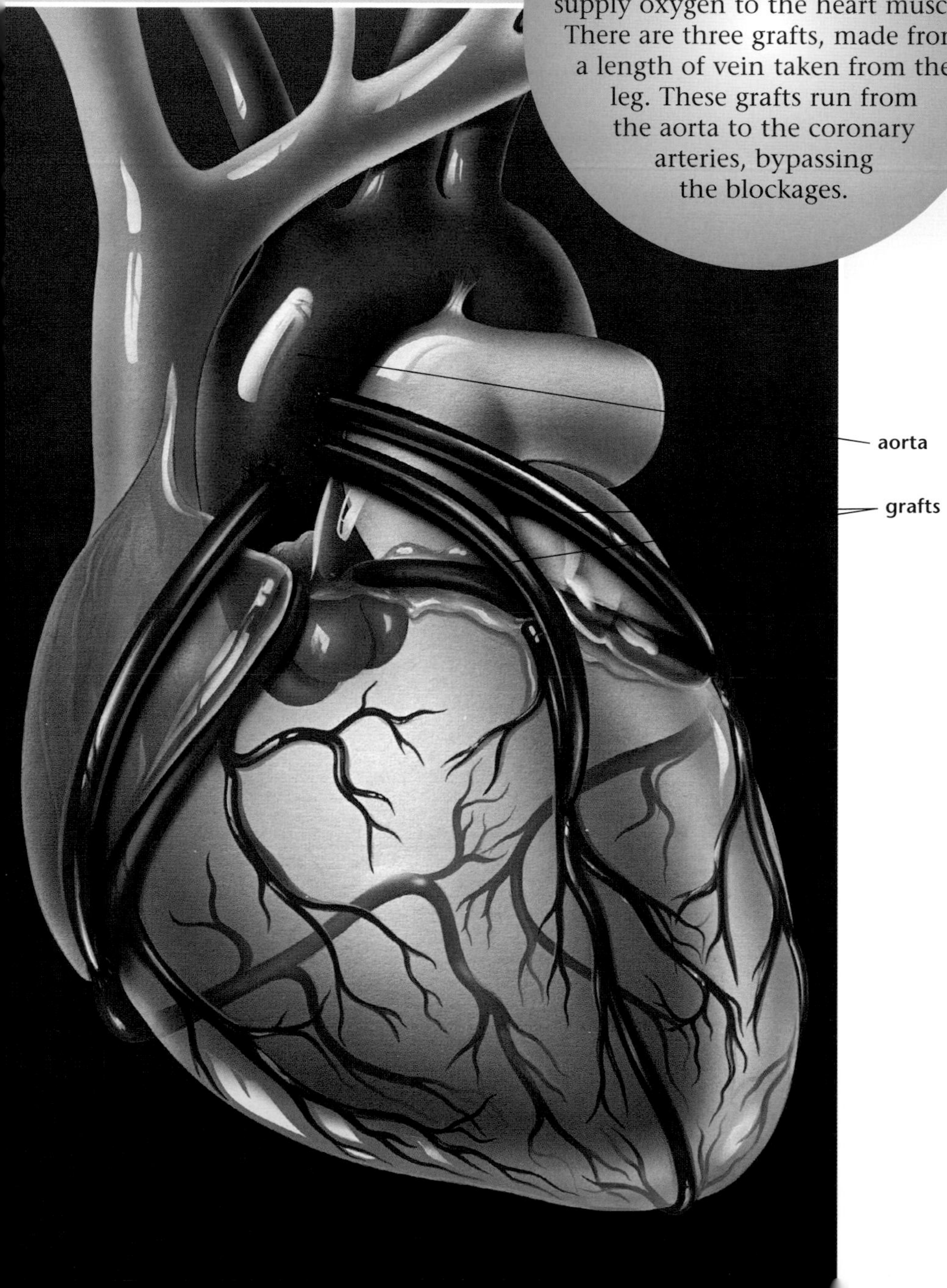

aorta

grafts

In the future, it may be possible to treat a diseased heart with a simple stem cell transplant. Healthy heart tissue grown in the laboratory would be transplanted directly into the patient's diseased heart. Growing tissues in the laboratory is called tissue engineering.

This is a magnetic resonance image (MRI) brain scan of a person suffering from MS. The red and yellow areas on the left show damage to the sheaths around the nerve fibres. This damage causes symptoms such as speech problems and paralysis.

HOW CAN STEM CELLS HELP PEOPLE WITH MS?

Multiple sclerosis (MS) is a disease in which the patient's own body attacks the protective sheaths surrounding their nerve cells. MS is caused by a fault in the **immune system**. Researchers have been investigating whether patients can be helped by having a bone marrow transplant. Bone marrow stem cells are taken from the patient and grown in the laboratory. Then the patient has **chemotherapy** to destroy their immune system and the stem cells are injected into the bloodstream. Although this treatment does not cure the disease, it is hoped that the stem cells will slow it down or stop it getting worse.

Treating Parkinson's disease

Parkinson's disease is caused by the loss of nerve cells in a particular area of the brain. These cells produce dopamine, a chemical messenger that transmits signals within the brain. If there is not enough dopamine some nerve cells fail to work properly and the person is unable to control their movements normally. Parkinson's disease was first described in detail by a British doctor, James Parkinson, in 1817. Symptoms of Parkinson's appear gradually, but get worse and worse. They include trembling, difficulty with balance, stiff arms and legs, and slowness of movement.

It is impossible to know who will get Parkinson's or to prevent it from occurring. Most people who get it are over 50 but there are some young sufferers too. On average, about 1 person in 500 gets Parkinson's disease. Among the sufferers are well-known people such as the actor Michael J. Fox, boxer Muhammad Ali, and former United States Attorney General Janet Reno. There is no cure for Parkinson's disease. But there are medicines that can help patients to manage the symptoms. However, as the disease gets worse, stronger and stronger drugs are required. These may have unpleasant side-effects, such as mental confusion.

In 1998, American actor Michael J. Fox announced that he was retiring from acting as he had been diagnosed with Parkinson's. In 2000 he set up a research foundation dedicated to finding a cure for the disease.

DENNIS TURNER'S STORY

During the late 1990s, Dr. Dennis Turner was suffering from the usual symptoms of Parkinson's disease. He expected to be on strong drugs for the rest of his life and probably to be confined to a wheelchair as the disease progressed. However his neurosurgeon, Dr. Michel F. Levesque, carried out an amazing new procedure that involved using Dr. Turner's own stem cells. First, a pea-sized sample of tissue was removed from Dr. Turner's brain. The stem cells in this tissue sample were identified and isolated. Then they were grown in the laboratory so that there were millions of them. Finally, these stem cells were injected back into Dr. Turner's brain. A year later, the symptoms of Parkinson's were greatly reduced. Turner testified in 2004 before the US Senate, "*My trembling grew less and less, until to all appearances it was gone.*"

Stem cells may eventually be used to treat Parkinson's. One possible technique is the use of embryonic stem cells in the brain, to replace the missing cells. However, this is very controversial as it uses embryonic stem cells. Another line of research involves using adult stem cells taken from the patient's own brain.

Stem cell therapy is not yet available to most Parkinson's patients. This patient is undergoing neurosurgery to implant electrodes in her brain. The hope is that the electrodes will stimulate the nerve cells and stop her limbs from trembling.

Stem cells and cancer

Cancer is one of the biggest killers of people in the developed world. Treatment can involve the use of powerful drugs and recovery times can be long. Stem cells could speed up recovery. However, there are concerns that stem cells might also cause cancer.

A cancer is caused when cells grow and divide uncontrollably, creating a growth called a **tumour**. To treat the cancer successfully, the tumour has to be removed quickly, before any of the cancerous cells detach and move around the body in the bloodstream. It is hard to be sure exactly why a cell starts dividing in this uncontrolled way. It could be a result of genetics or from chemical pollutants, such as tar from smoking cigarettes.

Treating cancer

The treatment used partly depends on the size of the tumour. If the tumour is not too large it can be removed by surgery. Sometimes a tumour can be treated using **radiation** to kill the cancer cells.

If the cancerous tumour is small, doctors may treat it using radiotherapy. This damages the cancer cells so they stop growing and dividing and the tumour shrinks.

The other form of treatment is **chemotherapy**. This involves pumping powerful chemicals into the bloodstream. These chemicals then circulate around the body, destroying cancer cells. Patients suffering from blood cancers like **leukaemia** have chemotherapy, followed by a bone marrow transplant to replace the cells. Doctors have also started using **transfusions** of **umbilical cord** blood to supply the stem cells.

These rounded cancerous cells look very like stem cells. However, unlike stem cells, cancerous cells divide in an uncontrolled manner, producing a tumour.

Could stem cells cause cancer?

Like cancer cells, stem cells divide repeatedly. With stem cells, this happens in a controlled way. However, scientists are worried that stem cells might sometimes go out of control and start causing cancer when they are injected into a patient.

Now that stem cells can be grown in the laboratory, scientists can observe them over long periods of time. They have found that the stem cells gradually gain abnormal **chromosomes**. It would not be safe to transplant an abnormal cell into a patient, as it could end up causing a cancer.

HOW DOES CHEMOTHERAPY WORK?

Chemotherapy involves treating a patient with powerful drugs that attack the rapidly dividing cells that cause cancer. However, the drugs also attack other dividing cells, such as those in the stomach lining and in hair follicles. The drugs can therefore cause nasty side-effects, such as nausea and hair loss. Chemotherapy also harms the rapidly dividing stem cells in the bone marrow. Injecting stem cells at the same time as the chemotherapy can lessen the side-effects and increase the chances of survival in children suffering from leukaemia.

A look into the future

People are researching **stem cells** in many laboratories around the world. This means that our understanding of stem cells and **regenerative medicine** is improving all the time. This knowledge may be useful in the fight against health problems such as heart disease, cancer, and diabetes.

Nanog

Scientists have long asked themselves why embryonic stem cells divide more than adult stem cells. The answer to this question may lie with a **protein** that has recently been found in embryonic stem cells taken from mice. The role of this protein is to keep the stem cells dividing. Ian Chambers, who discovered the protein, called it Nanog after the mythological Celtic land where everyone stays young forever. This protein has not been found in adult stem cells. Scientists suspect that this may be one of the reasons why adult stem cells do not divide as much as embryonic ones.

Now researchers know that Nanog exists, the next step is to try to find out how it works. It is hoped that this protein will enable scientists to find out why embryonic stem cells stop producing more stem cells and switch to producing specialized cells. Some scientists think that it may help them to understand the processes of aging in the body.

TALKING SCIENCE

"Nanog seems to be a master molecule that makes embryonic stem cells grow in the laboratory. In effect, this makes stem cells immortal. Being Scottish, I therefore chose the name after the Tirnan Og legend. If Nanog has the same effect in humans as we have found in mice, this will be a key step in developing embryonic stem cells for medical treatments."
Dr. Ian Chambers, BBC News website

In the future, stem cell research may enable doctors to repair the damage to this boy's spine, so that he can walk again.

Repairing the spine

Each year, thousands of people suffer injuries that leave them paralysed. Regenerative medicine researchers have injected stem cells into mice with injured spinal cords. After 16 weeks, the mice start to regain some of their ability to walk. However, this promising research has a long way to go before similar treatments could be used on human patients.

New teeth

Dentists routinely check for cancers in the mouth and throat when they examine somebody's teeth. Facial cancers can be very disfiguring, sometimes destroying the person's teeth, jawbone, and skin. At present, the face and jaw have to be rebuilt after cancer treatment, using metal plates and skin taken from other parts of the body. In the future, doctors hope to use a combination of X-rays, computer technology, and stem cells to design replacement bone and teeth for use in the reconstruction. Stem cells would be taken from the patient's skin and grown in the laboratory. The cells would be given a mixture of chemicals to make them turn into tissues such as bone, muscle, and fat.

Space science

A new technique is being used to produce large quantities of **umbilical cord** stem cells. It uses microgravity technology originally developed by NASA for the International Space Station. The cells are grown in a tiny chamber, called a bioreactor, that is just 40 millimetres long and can sit in the palm of someone's hand. The spinning mechanism in the reactor keeps the cells floating, just as if they were in space and there was no gravity. This method encourages stem cells to grow and divide. It also avoids the need to grow human embryonic stem cells on a bed of animal cells.

Turning back the clock

Adult stem cells are not very numerous. Scientists are therefore investigating ways of turning ordinary adult cells into stem cells, such as making a muscle cell into a stem cell. This would be a bit like turning back the clock, as all cells started life as stem cells. If this were possible, doctors would be able to take cells from a patient and convert them into stem cells. They could then use these stem cells to treat the patient. This process has been likened to the regeneration seen in animals such as lizards and starfish.

Humans, like this astronaut on a space walk, find it harder to function in zero-gravity conditions but embryonic stem cells respond well to a lack of gravity. These conditions encourage them to multiply.

"The idea is that eventually you could replace just about any tissue that is damaged. There are animals that regenerate whole tissues, such as salamanders that can grow new tails. Why can they and why can't we?"
Dr. Carlos M. Isales, Chief of Regenerative Medicine at the Medical College of Georgia, USA

This is an artist's fantasy image of "people turning back their biological clocks" but stem cell research could make this idea a reality.

One of the reasons why we age is that our cells do not replace themselves any more. They stop dividing and the tissues are no longer repaired. This is why our bodies start to age. Researchers are hoping that stem cells can be used to stop the process of aging and prolong life. In the future it may be possible to inject stem cells into the bloodstream. They would travel around the body to different tissues, where they would settle down and start dividing to replace the worn-out cells.

Treating older people with stem cells could save vast amounts of money. Each year, billions of pounds are spent on treating diseases in older people. As the diseases cannot be cured, the patients have to be given drugs for life. For example, diabetics need a constant supply of insulin, while Parkinson's patients need to be given L-Dopa indefinitely. If these diseases could be treated with stem cell **transplants**, there would be massive savings.

Regenerative medicine today

Regenerative medicine and **stem cell** research have come a very long way in a short time. About 300 years ago, scientists could barely see a **cell**. Now cells can be studied in incredible detail and grown in the laboratory. Soon it may be possible to grow new tissues and organs for **transplants**. The new field of regenerative medicine promises to use stem cells to extend our lifespan by replacing worn-out body parts and curing diseases.

However, doctors still need to be able to:

- grow healthy stem cells in the laboratory
- produce sufficient quantities of tissue for many transplants
- control the growth of stem cells so that they produce the right type of specialized cell
- ensure that the stem cells survive in the patient after transplant
- make sure that the new stem cells become part of the surrounding tissue after transplant
- ensure that the stem cells will work properly for the rest of the patient's life
- make sure that the stem cells will not harm the patient.

Forty years ago, McCulloch and Till could never have imagined how important their discovery was going to be. Who would have thought that a simple stem cell could capture the imagination of scientists, doctors, politicians, and the public and have such an important influence on our lives?

TALKING SCIENCE

"If you want to know when there will be a clinical impact on the field of diabetes, let's say, I can't answer that question; but I can answer the question, 'will there be a clinical impact?' Yes, there will be. I'm absolutely certain of it..."
Professor Roger Pederson, 2005, BBC News website

However, not all scientists think that stem cells will provide a miracle cure for disease and aging. Lord Robert Winston, Professor of Fertility at Imperial College, London, believes that the ability of stem cells to cure diseases has been exaggerated.

Other scientists are more confident. For instance, Roger Pederson, Professor of Regenerative Medicine at the University of Cambridge, UK, is certain that stem cells will enable drug companies to make big advances, as they will be able to test their drugs on specific types of cells.

Lord Robert Winston has been involved with fertility research since the 1970s. He founded the British National Health Service **in vitro fertilization (IVF)** programme in 1981.

TALKING SCIENCE

"The study of stem cells is one of the most exciting areas in biology but I think it is unlikely that embryonic stem cells are likely to be useful in healthcare for a long time."
Lord Robert Winston, 2005, BBC News website

Timeline

1595 Dutchman Zacharias Janssen builds first microscope.

1665 Englishman Robert Hooke publishes Micrographia, a book of all his studies using the microscope. It is filled with illustrations, all drawn by Hooke.

1674 Dutchman Anton van Leeuwenhoek becomes the first person to describe red blood cells as seen under the microscope, followed by sperm cells in 1677.

1683 Anton van Leeuwenhoek looks at bacteria under a microscope.

1920s Frenchman Louis de Broglie studies the movement of electrons, while Hans Busch discovers that magnets can focus an electron beam on to an object.

1932 Max Knoll and Ernst Ruska in Germany build the first transmission electron microscope (TEM).

1951 First scanning electron microscope (SEM) is built by the Englishman Sir Charles Oatley.

1958 Frenchman Jean Dausset discovers that cells have antigens on their cell membrane that help the immune system to identify the body's own cells.

1963 Ernest McCulloch and James Till publish their work on bone marrow and stem cells.

1968 First successful bone marrow transplant between non-identical siblings takes place at the University of Minnesota, USA.

1973 First successful bone marrow transplant takes place between a donor and a patient who was not closely related to the donor.

1974 American Dr. Gail Martin, at University College, London, works out how to keep fragile stem cells alive in a dish so that scientists can study their unique characteristics.

1981 Dr. Martin Evans and Dr. Matthew Kaufman, working at the University of Cambridge, discover embryonic stem cells in mice. In the same year, similar results are reported by Dr. Gail Martin, now working at University of California, San Francisco.

1981 The term "stem cell" is used for the first time by Gail Martin.

1990 Dr. E. Donnall Thomas is awarded the Nobel Prize in Medicine for his pioneering work in transplantation.

1998 Two research teams, one led by James Thomson and the other led by John Gearhart, manage to grow stem cells in the laboratory.

1999 Dr. Michel F. Levesque injects stem cells into the brain of Dr. Turner, a patient suffering from Parkinson's disease. The stem cells had been taken from Dr. Turner's own brain and grown in the laboratory before being put back into his brain.

2001 Researchers at the University of California, Los Angeles, and the University of Pittsburgh extract stem cells from fat removed from the body using liposuction.

2005 Stem cells found in the blood of the umbilical cord and in the placenta.

2005 Scientists use microgravity techniques to grow stem cells in tiny bioreactors.

2005 British eye specialist Mr. Sheraz Daya restores the sight of 40 patients with damaged corneas, using human stem cells grown in a laboratory and transplanted on to the eye.

Biographies

These are some of the leading scientists in the story of regenerative medicine.

Martin Evans

Martin Evans graduated from the University of Cambridge in 1963 and gained his doctorate at University College, London. In 1978, he returned to the University of Cambridge, where he worked with Dr. Matthew Kaufman. In 1981, they discovered embryonic stem cells in mice. In 1999, he moved to Cardiff University, where he is Professor of Mammalian Genetics. He is a Fellow of the Royal Society, and in 2003 he was given a knighthood for his services to medical science.

John Gearhart

John Gearhart's father died when he was only six, and Gearhart spent the following 10 years in an orphanage. He went to Pennsylvania State University with the aim of studying horticulture but decided to do genetics instead. He got a master's degree from the University of New Hampshire in plant genetics, and a doctoral degree in genetics from Cornell University. For the past 20 years, he has studied the genetic disease, Down's Syndrome. This research led him to see the need for identifying and studying human stem cells. In 1998, he led the John Hopkins team that successfully grew human embryonic stem cells. Dr. Gearhart is currently Professor of Gynecology and Obstetrics and of Physiology at the Johns Hopkins University School of Medicine, USA.

Robert Hooke (1635–1703)

Robert Hooke was born on the Isle of Wight, England. As well as making discoveries in the world of biology, he was a great scientist and invented many scientific instruments, including the spirit level, barometer, and hypodermic needle. He also devised laws of physics such as Hooke's Law. The results of his observations using the microscope were published in *Micrographia* in 1665. He was the first person to use the word "cell". After the Great Fire of London in 1666, he worked with his friend Sir Christopher Wren to rebuild the city of London.

Anton van Leeuwenhoek (1632–1723)

Anton van Leeuwenhoek has been called the father of microbiology. He built his own microscopes, some of which were able to magnify objects 270 times. He lived in Holland. Although he never attended a university and never had formal scientific training, he made some astounding discoveries. He was the first scientist ever to give a detailed description of red blood cells (1675) and human sperm cells (1677) or to see bacteria (1683). Van Leeuwenhoek made his discoveries known in letters to Europe's leading scientific societies. Over 50 years, he wrote more than 300 such letters, many of which were published.

Ernest McCulloch and James Till

Ernest McCulloch trained to be a doctor but during the late 1950s he switched to research on radiation and cancer. In 1957, James Till obtained a PhD in Biophysics from Yale and joined McCulloch's laboratory at the Ontario Cancer Institute as the expert in radiation measurement. In the early 1960s, the two scientists started a series of experiments that involved injecting bone marrow cells into mice that had been given radiation treatment to kill the cells in their bone marrow. In 1963, they published their results demonstrating the presence of stem cells. Later that year, they published evidence that stem cells could renew themselves.

Both scientists continued to work in this field. In 1974, McCulloch became a Fellow of the Royal Society of Canada, and in 1999 he was made a Fellow of the Royal Society of London. In 2004, he joined the Canadian Medical Hall of Fame. He holds the distinguished title of University Professor Emeritus at the University of Toronto, Canada. In 2005, McCulloch and Till were awarded the Albert Lasker Award for Basic Medical Research (the American equivalent of the Nobel Prize).

Dr. E. Donnall Thomas

In 1990, Dr. E. Donnall Thomas was awarded the Nobel Prize in Medicine for his pioneering work in transplantation. Dr. Donnall Thomas first became interested in bone marrow and leukaemia while he was at medical school in the 1940s. However, he did not start his pioneering work on bone marrow transplants using dogs until 1955. During the early to mid-1970s, Dr. Thomas performed more than 100 transplants for patients with aplastic anaemia and leukaemia, using brothers and sisters as the donors. He was awarded the Nobel Prize because of his successful research in both clinical and experimental bone marrow transplantation.

James Thomson

In 1981, James Thomson graduated with a BSc in biophysics from the University of Illinois, USA. He received his doctorate in veterinary medicine in 1985, and his doctorate in molecular biology in 1988. His research was concerned with early development in mammals. In 1990, he moved to the University of Wisconsin, where he carried out pioneering work on isolating and growing embryonic stem cells. In 1995, his team was the first to isolate stem cells from a non-human primate. Then, in 1998, the team successfully isolated and grew human embryonic stem cells. James Thomson is Professor of Anatomy at the University of Wisconsin Medical School.

Glossary

Alzheimer's disease incurable disease that destroys brain cells, gradually causing extreme personality changes

antigen substance, foreign to the body, that stimulates the production of antibodies by the immune system, such as viruses and bacteria

antibody protein produced by white blood cells that recognizes and helps fight infections

artery major vessel that carries blood away from the heart

atom smallest component of an element that has the chemical properties of the element

axon long, fibre-like extension of a nerve cell that carries an electrical signal

bacterium/bacteria single-celled organism that does not have a nucleus

bone marrow liquid-like tissue found in the centre of the body's largest bones

cell basic building block of an organism, containing a nucleus and cytoplasm

chemotherapy treating cancer with chemicals that seek out and destroy cancerous cells

chromosome thread-like structure in the nucleus, made up of DNA and protein

clone identical copy of an organism

cornea clear part of the eye, that lets light into the eye

cytoplasm jelly-like substance that fills a cell

dendrite tiny extension that carries the electrical signal towards the cell body of a nerve cell

DNA (deoxyribonucleic acid) molecule that carries the body's genetic information

electron negatively charged particle that moves around the nucleus of an atom

electron microscope microscope that uses a beam of electrons, rather than light, to magnify an object

embryo new individual that forms when an egg is fertilized

fetus in humans, term to describe the unborn baby from the eighth week of pregnancy to birth

gene unit of inheritance that is passed on from parent to offspring

haemoglobin protein found in red blood cells, which picks up oxygen

hormone chemical messenger in the body

immune system body's system of defences against disease

IVF (in vitro fertilization) process in which a woman's egg is fertilized in a glass dish in a laboratory

leukaemia cancer of the blood which affects white blood cells

light microscope type of microscope that uses light to magnify an image

liposuction process in which fatty tissue is sucked out of the body

medium substance containing nutrients, in which cells or bacteria can be cultured or grown

membrane thin barrier around a cell or organelle

mitochondrion/mitochondria organelle found in most cells, which generates most of the cell's energy

mitosis growth division in which one cell divides to form two identical cells

molecule smallest particle of a substance that retains the properties of the substance

multiple sclerosis (MS) disease that damages the fatty layer covering most nerve cells

nucleus central part of the cell which contains DNA and controls many cell functions

organelle microscopic structure in a cell, such as the nucleus

organism living being

placenta organ linking the mother with the fetus in the uterus

plasma liquid part of the blood in which the blood cells float

platelet type of blood cell that is responsible for blood clotting

protein large molecule made from amino acids

protozoa single-celled organism

radiation energy released as particles or electromagnetic waves. Sources include medical X-rays.

regenerative medicine medical field specializing in rebuilding parts of the body using cells and tissues

rejection reaction by the immune system to the presence of a transplanted organ or tissue

scanning electron microscope type of electron microscope in which the electrons bounce off the surface of an object, allowing surface features to be studied

sperm cell male sex cell

spleen organ of the body that produces some white blood cells, filters the blood, stores blood cells, and destroys old blood cells

stem cell cell that retains the ability to divide and to form specialized cells such as blood cells

transfusion transfer of blood or blood products from one individual to another

transplant when living tissues are removed from one part of the body, or another body, and placed in another

tumour cancerous growth

umbilical cord structure that links the fetus with the placenta. Blood vessels within the umbilical cord carry nutrients from the placenta.

uterus (also called the womb) female organ in which the fetus (unborn child) grows and develops

Further resources

If you have enjoyed this book and want to find out more, you can look at the following books and websites.

Books

21st Century Citizen: Genetic Engineering
Paul Dowswell
(Franklin Watts, 2004)

Genetic Engineering: The Facts
Sally Morgan
(Evans Brothers, 2002)

Science at the Edge: Body Sculpting,
Sally Morgan
(Heinemann Library, 2004)

Science at the Edge: Cloning
Sally Morgan
(Heinemann Library, 2002)

Science at the Edge: Frontiers of Surgery
Ann Fullick
(Heinemann Library, 2005)

Websites

Stem Cell Information
stemcells.nih.gov
The official National Institutes of Health resource for stem cell research.

Genetic Science Learning Centre
gslc.genetics.utah.edu
An excellent website with information on all aspects of biotechnology including stem cells, explained with diagrams and photos.

Biotechnology online
www.biotechnologyonline.gov. au
An Australian resource for biotechnology for secondary school pupils.

Bioscience Information Gateway for the European Public and Information Practitioners
www.ecod-bio.org/main.htm
A website that provides information on biosciences, answers to many frequently asked questions, and good-quality educational material.

Index

Index

Titles in the *Chain Reactions* series include:

Hardback   0 431 18593 X

Hardback   0 431 18594 8

Hardback   0 431 18595 6

Hardback   0 431 18596 4

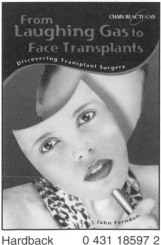

Hardback   0 431 18597 2

Hardback   0 431 18598 0

Find out about other titles from Heinemann Library on our website www.heinemann.co.uk/library